Arranging in the Digital World

Techniques for Arranging Popular Music Using Today's Electronic and Digital Instruments

Corey Allen

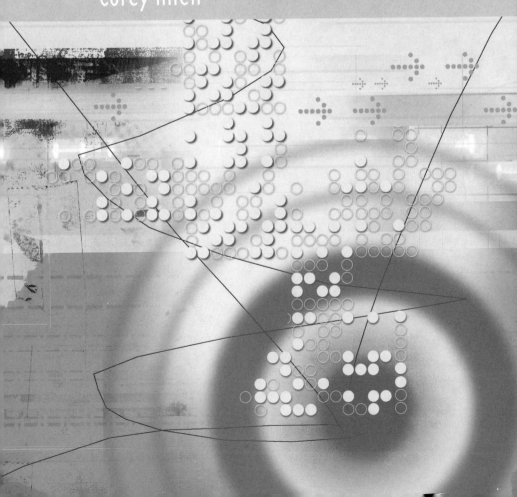

Berklee Press

Director: Dave Kusek
Managing Editor: Debbie Cavalier
Marketing Manager: Ola Frank
Sr. Writer/Editor: Jonathan Feist

ISBN 0-634-00634-7

1140 Boylston Street
Boston, MA 02215-3693 USA
(617) 747-2146

Visit Berklee Press Online at
www.berkleepress.com

DISTRIBUTED BY

HAL•LEONARD®
CORPORATION
7777 W. BLUEMOUND RD. P.O. BOX 13819
MILWAUKEE, WISCONSIN 53213

Visit Hal Leonard Online at
www.halleonard.com

CONTENTS

INTRODUCTION

This book is for people who want to make more authentic-sounding digital arrangements. The techniques in this book are useful to:

- **Music teachers:** either private instructors or those who teach band, orchestra, chorus, general music, ear training, music appreciation, music history, arranging, or composition, or those who just want better-sounding examples for rhythmic drills or style analysis.

- **Church musicians** who want to enhance their traveling ministries or invigorate accompaniments for their church services.

- **Gigging musicians** who would like to produce a repertoire of "CD ready" songs that can be performed live.

- **People for whom music is a passion**.

The purpose of this book is not to prepare you for a career as a professional arranger or an orchestrator. Our focus will be on sequencing techniques for the digital arranger rather than on actual writing techniques. The presumption is that you will sequence your own arrangements and they will be performed by you and your digital keyboard. I will give you tips on how to sequence more efficiently and how to make your virtual instrumental tracks sound more authentic. New terms requiring definitions are *italicized*. Definitions for the terms can be found in the glossary in the back of the book.

I would like to thank Debbie Cavalier at Berklee Press for the opportunity to write this book, Tom Miller at Kurzweil Music Systems for his support, and Tom McCauley for his technical advice. I would also like to thank the teachers I had when I was a student at the Berklee College of Music for providing me with a very solid musical education, which prepared me well for a life as a professional musician. Lastly, I would like to thank my family for their help, love, and support while I wrote this book.

CHAPTER I
Definitions for the Digital Arranger

For the purposes of this book, I'll define arrangement as a setting of a piece of music—typically a song—for a group of instruments or voices. The choice of just which group of instruments or voices to use is up to the arranger. Since a comprehensive study of arranging is well beyond the scope of this book, we'll concern ourselves with arranging popular music for digital instruments and concentrate on terminology and practices that pertain thereto.

Sequencer: A sequencer is a digital recording device that records a numeric sequence of events—data, NOT SOUND. A sequencer customarily takes one of three forms:

1. A piece of software used in conjunction with a computer that manages and stores the digital information you input from a keyboard or a computer.

2. A stand-alone device.

3. A component of a digital keyboard. Such keyboards are often called "workstations" or "digital ensembles" because they incorporate the ability to record various sounds on multiple tracks.

Multi-timbral keyboards used in conjunction with sequencers make it possible to produce inexpensive, professional-sounding arrangements. But they don't guarantee that your arrangement will sound "right." I will show you some practical sequencing techniques that will help enliven your digital arrangements.

There are a few demands made of the digital arranger that aren't expected of arrangers of acoustic instruments. For example, digital arrangers have to understand the way diverse instruments are actually played in order to create a believable representation of them from a keyboard. As a digital arranger, you'll also have to understand the technical abilities and limitations of the particular *software* and *hardware* you have at your disposal. You'll have to learn some basic MIDI concepts and a few production techniques that will help make your digital arrangements sound great. Let's begin by defining a few terms.

MIDI: MIDI is an acronym for Musical Instrument Digital Interface. It is simply a number system of 128 increments that places a value from 0 to 127 on every aspect of digital music. From the choice of sound you want to play to the recording process, everything has a number from 0 to 127 associated with it. MIDI allows computers to process this numeric data as any other data and send it to digital instruments that translate it into musical terms and respond appropriately.

MIDI Channel: Think of a MIDI channel as a stream in which digital information flows. You must choose the direction you want the stream to flow—from your synthesizer to your sequencer when you're recording, and from your sequencer to your synthesizer when you're listening to what you've recorded. MIDI is comprised of 16 separate channels. On a multi-timbral synthesizer, a different sound can be assigned to each MIDI channel.

Bank Select: As mentioned above, the MIDI numbering system is based on 128. But many digital instruments have hundreds of sounds to choose from. How do you select *patch number* 129 if there are only 128 MIDI numbers? The answer is that sounds, also called *programs,* can be organized in groups called banks. Banks usually contain 100 programs. So, you would choose patch number 256 by selecting bank number 2, patch number 56.

Track: Remember, a sequencer doesn't record sound, only numbers that tell a digital instrument things like what notes to play, what sounds (programs) to use, and how loud to be. This data is stored and ordered as a straight line of information called a track. In order to use your sequencer to record or play back music on your digital keyboard, each track must be assigned a specific MIDI channel. If you're using a sequencer that is built into a digital keyboard, MIDI channel assignments usually look like this: Track 1 goes to MIDI Channel 1, Track 2 goes to MIDI Channel 2, and so on. Later, we will explore some reasons why you may want to assign different tracks to different MIDI channel numbers.

General MIDI: General MIDI (GM) is a set of standards agreed upon by all of the leading digital instrument manufacturers. By standardizing a sound-set and establishing fixed technical boundaries, GM gives you the flexibility to create a sequence on one GM-compatible instrument and perform it on another. Before the GM standard, a MIDI arrangement created on one keyboard would sound completely different when played back on another. All of the musical examples on the accompanying disk are in the General MIDI format. Whether your sound source is a digital keyboard or a stand-alone tone generator, look for this emblem to determine if your equipment is General MIDI compatible:

Fig. 1.1. General MIDI Logo

The General MIDI sounds and respective *program (patch)* numbers are listed below.

General MIDI Sound Set

1: GrandPno	33: WoodBass	65: SprnoSax	97: Rain
2: BritePno	34: FngrBass	66: AltoSax	.98: SoundTrk
3: El.Grand	35: PickBass	67: TenorSax	99: Crystal
4: HnkyTonk	36: Fretless	68: BariSax	100: Atmosphr
5: ElPiano1	37: SlapBas1	69: Oboe	101: Bright
6: ElPiano2	38: SlapBas2	70: EnglHorn	102: Goblin
7: Harpsich	39: SynBass1	71: Bassoon	103: Echoes
8: Clavinet	40: SynBass2	72: Clarinet	104: SciFi
9: Celesta	41: Violin	73: Piccolo	105: Sitar
10: Glocken	42: Viola	74: Flute	106: Banjo
11: MusicBox	43: Cello	75: Recorder	107: Shamisen
12: Vibes	44: Contra	76: PanFlute	108: Koto
13: Marimba	45: TremStrg	77: Bottle	109: Kalimba
14: Xylophon	46: Pizzicto	78: Shakuchi	110: Bagpipe
15: TubulBel	47: Harp	79: Whistle	111: Fiddle
16: Dulcimer	48: Timpani	80: Ocarina	112: Shanai
17: DrawOrgan	49: Ensmble1	81: SquareLd	113: TnklBell
18: PercOrgn	50: Ensmble2	82: SawLd	114: Agogo
19: RockOrgn	51: SynStrg1	83: CaliopLd	115: StlDrum
20: ChrcOrgan	52: SynStrg2	84: ChiffLd	116: WoodBlok
21: ReedOrgn	53: AahChoir	85: CharanLd	117: TaikoDrm
22: Acordion	54: OohChoir	86: VoiceLd	118: MelodTom
23: Harmnica	55: SynChoir	87: FifthLd	119: SynthTom
24: TangoAcd	56: OrchHit	88: Bass&Ld	120: RevCymbl
25: NylonGtr	57: Trumpet	89: NewAgePd	121: FretNoiz
26: SteelGtr	58: Trombone	90: WarmPd	122: BrthNoiz
27: JazzGtr	59: Tuba	91: PolysynPd	123: Seashore
28: CleanGtr	60: MuteTrum	92: ChoirPd	124: Tweet
29: MuteGtr	61: FrenchHr	93: BowedPd	125: Telphone
30: Ovrdrive	62: BrasSect	94: MetalPd	126: Helicptr
31: Distortd	63: SynBras1	95: HaloPd	127: Applause
32: Harmnics	64: SynBras2	96: SweepPd	128: Gunshot

Fig. 1.2. General MIDI Sound Set

Consult your owner's manual to learn how to put your keyboard or *tone generator* into the GM mode.

Measures/Beats/Ticks: These are the units of measurement we use to identify our location in a sequence. "Measure" refers to the exact bar number. "Beat" refers to a specific beat within the bar. "Tick" is a subdivision of a single beat. Sequencers usually divide a single beat into 480 ticks. The number 480 is easily divisible into equal parts and, therefore, very convenient. For example, in 4/4 time:

480 ticks = 1 quarter note

240 ticks = 1 eighth note

160 ticks = 1 eighth-note triplet

120 ticks = 1 sixteenth note

80 ticks = 1 sixteenth-note triplet

A typical sequencer screen looks like this:

Fig. 1.3. Sequencer Screen

In this example, we're at measure 5, on beat 3, on tick 360.

CHALLENGE

What musical part of the beat does the tick 360 represent? The answer is at the end of this chapter.

Interface: A single device or a combination of software and hardware working in conjunction with one another that acts as a translator between your multi-timbral digital instrument and your sequencer.

Now that you have working definitions for some of the technical terms you'll use as a digital arranger, let's define a couple of useful musical terms.

Style: The musical landscape in which you set your song. Your choice of style very often dictates the instrumentation you'll use and is influenced by many considerations, such as who your audience is and who the performer will be.

Groove: The feel with which the rhythm section will play your arrangement: i.e., a samba groove, a swing groove, or a 6/8 gospel groove.

ANSWER

The tick 360 is the fourth sixteenth note of a beat. Therefore, the musical representation of the above diagram is:

Ex. 1.1.

CHAPTER II
Style and Instrumentation

Style and instrumentation go hand in hand. Each style of music implies a specific instrumentation. One naturally expects to find a drum set and an acoustic bass in a jazz combo, or a five-string banjo in a bluegrass band. Conversely, you would not expect to hear a bagpipe in a string orchestra. As an arranger, one of your most important jobs is to know which instruments are typically used in any style of music.

To develop your instrument awareness, listen carefully to various styles of music and take notice of—even take notes on—which instruments are playing. Let me get you started by listing a few styles and their most standard instrumentation:

- **Pop:** Rhythm Section (piano, synthesizer, bass, guitar, and drum set), Background Vocals, Strings

- **Jazz:** Rhythm Section, Brass, Background Vocals

- **Rock:** Rhythm Section, Brass, Strings, Background Vocals

- **Latin/Brazilian:** Rhythm Section, Background Vocals, Brass, Percussion, Strings

- **Country:** Rhythm Section, Background Vocals, Brass, Strings

- **Orchestral:** Strings, Woodwinds, Brass, Percussion

RHYTHM SECTION

The rhythm section is used in almost every form of popular music and is usually comprised of piano/keyboard, acoustic or electric bass, acoustic or electric guitar, drums, percussion, or some variation thereof. Of course, how these instruments are played individually and in an ensemble vary from style to style. Let's take a look at each instrument individually and then learn some of their typical *licks* in a few common styles.

Writing for the Rhythm Section

DRUM SET

The drum set or "trap set" is actually a collection of different drums and cymbals arranged so they can all be played by one player. Although there are many variations, the customary configuration is:

- **Bass Drum:** played by the drummer's right foot, used mostly for accenting beginnings and endings of phrases and important melodic events.

- **Snare Drum:** has metal wires along the bottom skin that gives it its unique sound. Originally a marching drum, it's the highest-pitched drum in the set and is played with either sticks or brushes. Used mostly for keeping time and accenting strong melodic points.

- **Hi-Hat Cymbal:** played by the drummer's left foot as well as with sticks, used mostly to accent beats 2 and 4.

- **Ride Cymbal:** played with either sticks or brushes, it's used to keep time with a steady rhythmic *ostinato*.

- **Crash Cymbal:** used mostly for emphasis and to punctuate phrases. It is usually played with sticks.

- **Floor Tom-tom:** pitched a little higher than the bass drum, played with either sticks or brushes, used mostly for fills into a new phrase.

- **Mounted Tom-tom:** usually mounted on the side of the bass drum, it's pitched a little higher than the floor tom-tom and played with either sticks or brushes. Used mostly for fills into a new phrase.

Figure 2.1 indicates the keys on your keyboard that correspond to the drum sounds listed above in the General MIDI sound set.

Since the GM sound set was designed to be a "common denominator," you'll probably discover other drum sounds which are not part of the GM soundset that may sound more appealing. Be sure to write down their *patch number* so you'll be able to find them in a hurry if you need to.

NOTE	General MIDI Drum Map
C2	Kick Drum 1
	Side Stick
	Snare Drum 1
	Hand Clap
	Snare Drum 2
	Low Tom 2
	Closed High-hat (EXC1)
	Low Tom 1
	Pedal High-hat (EXC1)
	Mid Tom 2
	Open High-hat 2 (EXC1)
B2	Mid Tom 1
	High Tom 2
C3	Crash Cymbal 1
	High Tom 1
	Ride Cymbal 1
	Chinese Cymbal
	Ride Bell
	Tambourine
	Splash Cymbal
	Cowbell
	Crash Cymbal 2
	Vibra-slap
B3	Ride Cymbal 2
	High Bongo
C4	Low Bongo
	Mute High Conga
	Open High Conga
	Low Conga
	High Timbale
	Low Timbale
	High Agogo
	Low Agogo
	Cabasa
	Maracas
B4	Short High Whistle (EXC2)
	Long Low Whistle (EXC2)
C5	Short Guiro (EXC3)
	Long Guiro (EXC3)
	Claves
	High Wood Block
	Low Wood Block
	Mute Cuica (EXC4)
	Open Cuica (EXC4)
	Mute Triangle (EXC5)
	Open Triangle (EXC5)
	Shaker
B5	Jingle Bell
	Bell Tree
C6	Castanets
	Mute Surdo (EXC6)
	Open Surdo (EXC6)

Fig. 2.1. General MIDI Percussion Keymap

DRUM SET PARTS

The role of the drummer first and foremost is to keep time. Good
drum parts indicate where phrases begin and end, emphasize important melodic notes, and use varying backgrounds in different sections
by slightly altering the beat pattern or using brushes in one section
and sticks in another. Example 2.1 illustrates the drum set notation
that will be used in this book. The clef used in this example is for non-
pitched instruments.

Ex. 2.1.

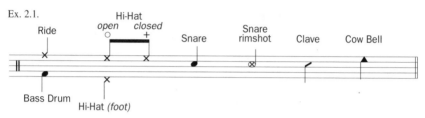

Swing

In a swing style, the drum set's most common rhythmic pattern is:

 Swing

Ex. 2.2.

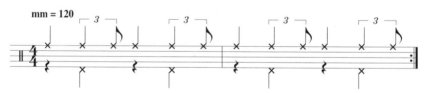

The ride cymbal plays the familiar ding-ding-a-ding, ding-a-ding
rhythm while the hi-hat keeps time on beats 2 and 4. Sometimes the
hi-hat plays the ride cymbal's rhythm and alternates between a *closed*
and an *open* sound.

An (o) written above a hi-hat note indicates that the note is to be
played open. A (+) written above the hi-hat note indicates that the note
is to be played closed.

Swing with Hi-Hat

Ex. 2.3.

The bass drum and snare drum are left to punctuate important points in the melody and mark the beginnings and ends of phrases.

Bossa Nova

In a bossa-nova style, the drum set's most common rhythmic pattern is:

 Bossa Nova Drum Pattern

Ex. 2.4.

Note: If this pattern were played on a real drum set, it would be executed entirely by the drummer's feet.

Jazz Waltz

In a jazz waltz style, the drum set's most common rhythmic pattern is:

 Jazz Waltz Drum Pattern

Ex. 2.5.

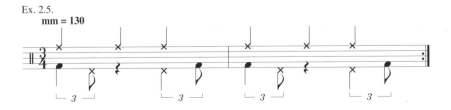

Samba

In a samba style, the drum set's most common rhythmic pattern is:

 Samba Drum Pattern

Ex. 2.6.

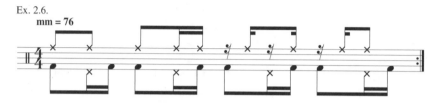

Pop

In a pop style, the drum set's two most common rhythmic patterns are:

 Pop-Style Rhythm 1 Drum Pattern

Ex. 2.7.

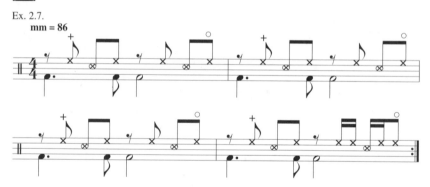

Notice the middle line of this drum part. Rather than a notehead there is an x with a circle around it. That means play the rim of the snare drum. Playing an attack on the rim of the drum gives the note a more metallic sound.

 Pop-Style Rhythm 2 Drum Pattern

Ex. 2.8.

BASS: ACOUSTIC AND ELECTRIC

For the purposes of this book, we'll assume that the acoustic bass, also known as the stand-up bass, the bass viol, the upright bass, and the doghouse, will be played *pizzicato,* meaning plucked, not *arco,* meaning played with a bow. It's important to remember when reading and notating bass parts that both the electric bass and the acoustic bass sound one octave lower than written. If the notes for these instruments were written at actual pitch, the number of *ledger lines* would be very cumbersome for the player to read. This is the written range for the bass:

Ex. 2.9. Written Bass Range

The acoustic bass is most commonly used in jazz settings and show music or when trying to imply an older, pre-electric style, such as turn-of-the-century dance music, including waltzes and fox trots. From a digital arranging point of view, electric bass can mean many different sounds depending on the style of music.

For example:

Electric Bass (GM Patch 34). Sounds like a note plucked with a finger. It can be short or long in duration.

Slap Bass (GM Patch 37). A percussive sound used for emphasis in rock, R&B and funk music.

Synth Bass or **Moog Bass** (GM Patch 40). Used in house, rap, techno, and '80s pop music.

BASS AND DRUM PARTS

In almost all cases, the bass drum part is closely related to the bass part. The following examples show how the bass and drums fit together across a variety of styles.

Samba

 Samba Bass and Drums

Ex. 2.10.

Swing

 Swing Bass and Drums

Ex. 2.11.

Pop

 Pop Bass and Drums

Ex. 2.12.

Funk

 Funk Bass and Drums

Ex. 2.13.

PIANO, ELECTRIC PIANO, KEYBOARD PARTS

I will assume that you are already familiar with the piano and have at least a basic level of keyboard technique. Listen to the MIDI files on the accompanying disk for audible examples of the following descriptions:

Acoustic Piano (GM Patch 1). Great for accompaniments and solos.

Rhodes Electric Piano (GM Patch 5). Great for *pads,* solos, and as the left-hand accompaniment for a right-hand acoustic piano lead line.

Synth Pads (GM Patch 90). Often used as a surrogate for string pads or by itself for a more modern pad foundation.

Synth Leads (GM Patch 82). Used for solos or counter lines.

ACOUSTIC GUITAR PARTS

Nylon String Guitar (GM Patch 25). Best used for a classical or Spanish-sounding effect.

Six-String or **Folk Guitar** (GM Patch 26). Great for country, folk, blues, soft rock, or any other musical style that employs a steel string, strumming sort of guitar sound.

Twelve-String Guitar (not part of the GM sound set). Great for folk or rock accompaniments.

Jazz Guitar (GM Patch 27). Good for Freddy Green swing-style playing, i.e., quarter-note "chunk, chunk, chunk."

ELECTRIC GUITAR PARTS

23 **Lead Electric Guitar** (GM Patch 31 or 30). Great for rock, blues leads, and solos.

24 **Muted Electric Guitar** (GM Patch 29). Single-note backgrounds. Great for R&B, pop, and jazz backgrounds.

25 **Stratocaster Guitar** (GM Patch 28). 12/8 chunk, early rock & roll.

PERCUSSION PARTS

Typically, the rhythm section is comprised of a keyboard instrument, bass, guitar, and drum set. Some styles of music require an expanded rhythm section that may include several other percussion instruments besides the drum set.

26 **Vibes** (GM Patch 12). Used for solos, as the left-hand accompaniment for keyboard or piano solos, or as pads.

Triangle. Most often used in bossa nova and samba styles. Less frequently used in pop styles. Just like hi-hat cymbals, the two sounds normally used are open and closed. Here is a typical pattern:

27 *Triangle*

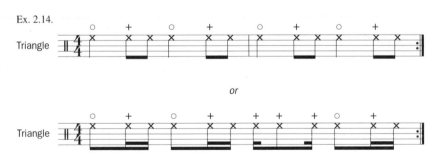

Ex. 2.14.

or

Shaker. Used in Brazilian, Latin, and some pop music. The shaker will almost always lend a Latin flavor to whatever style it's added. It normally plays a steady rhythm, lightly accenting the beat.

 Shaker

Ex. 2.15.

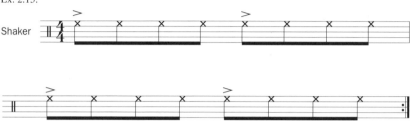

Conga Drums. Used mostly in Brazilian, Latin, pop, and jazz music. The most common configuration for conga drums is a set of two different drums that can produce several different pitches. With the GM sound set, your sound choices are low, open high, and mute high. Conga players also mute the drum by cupping their hand, which provides a short, choked sound. The most common conga pattern is called a mantaneo and is notated like this:

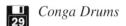 *Conga Drums*

Ex. 2.16.

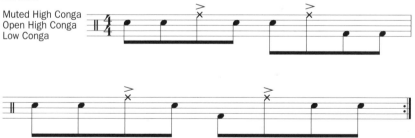

Bongo Drums. Used mostly in Brazilian, Latin, pop, jazz, and cabaret. They are usually played as a set of two drums pitched higher than congas. They are used to play fast, active passages.

 *Bongo Drums*

Ex. 2.17.

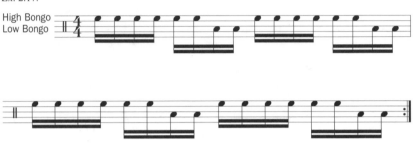

Cowbells. Used mostly in Brazilian, Latin, pop, and gospel styles. Cowbells usually keep time by accenting the first beat of the bar or every beat. However, in Latin music, their parts can get very complicated.

 Cowbells

Ex. 2.18.

Clave. The word "clave" has two meanings: A clave can be a percussion instrument or a specific two-bar rhythm pattern found in Latin music—particularly mambos. There are two basic rhythmic patterns, or claves, that act as the unifying rhythmic element in Latin music, and are, therefore, treated as sacrosanct. They are:

 Clave 1

Ex. 2.19a.

Clave 2

Ex. 2.19b.

Avoid changing or reversing the clave pattern after it has been established.

Tambourine. Used in Brazilian, Latin, pop, gospel, and classical styles of music. In pop music, the tambourine usually accents beats 2 and 4.

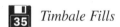 *Tambourine*

Ex. 2.20.

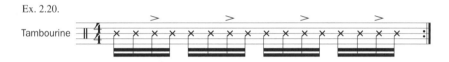

Timbales. Metal-sided drums that are most often heard playing fills at the ends of phrases.

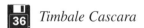 *Timbale Fills*

Timbales are often played in conjunction with suspended cymbals, which are attached to the side of the drum. A timbale player will often alternate playing the same rhythmic pattern on the cymbals or on the side of the timbales. That rhythmic pattern is called a cascara. A cascara is notated like this:

 *Timbale Cascara*

Ex. 2.21.

RHYTHM SECTION PARTS

Now let's look at a few different styles and see how these instruments play with one another within a rhythm section. The harmonic progressions or changes used in the following examples are representative of typical changes found in these styles.

Swing

 *Jazz Combo Swing*

Ex. 2.22.

*A common arranging technique with dominant seventh chords is to add "color notes" or "tensions" to the voicing. For example, the note E in the D7 chord is the 9th, and the note D in the F7 chord is the 13th.

Example 2.22 is a very traditional swing pattern. The guitar plays a very straight quarter-note rhythm. I would choose an acoustic guitar sound rather than an electric guitar sound for this pattern. Remember that the bass sounds one octave lower than it is written.

Bossa Nova

 Jazz Combo Bossa Nova

Ex. 2.23.

You can use either an electric or acoustic bass sound for bossa novas. Your choice should depend on how aggressive you want the sound of the style to be.

16-Beat Pop

39 *16-Beat Pop Ensemble*

Ex. 2.24.   **mm = 66**

An acoustic guitar part playing arpeggiated chords gives a sense of forward motion to this style. An electric piano sound is a little more full-sounding than an acoustic piano sound. I also used a pad to broaden the sound out even further.

Country

Notice the use of two different guitar sounds: electric and acoustic.
Also notice that the piano's arpeggio figure is providing all the forward motion.

40 *Country Band*

Ex. 2.25.   mm = 118

Bluegrass

Notice that there is no piano part.

 *Bluegrass Band*

Ex. 2.26.

Salsa

Notice the extended use of percussion instruments instead of a trap set.

 Salsa Ensemble

Ex. 2.27.

HINT: Learn which instruments are commonly used in the styles of music you like, find the programs on your digital keyboard that sound the most like them, and write down their numbers. This will save you a lot of time finding your favorite programs in the future.

CHAPTER III
How to Build an Arrangement

When I begin an arrangement, the first thing I consider is the form of the song. Knowing the song's form makes arranging decisions—such as when to change the harmony or instrumentation of a particular section—a lot easier. The form of the song will influence the way you develop your arrangement.

To determine a song's form, we need to look carefully at all of its individual elements: melody, harmony, rhythm, lyrics (if any), and the number of bars per section. For example, the song "Row, Row, Row Your Boat" has a two-part or *binary* form—each part being two bars long. The first two-bar phrase, called an *antecedent phrase,* sets up the second two-bar phrase called a *consequent phrase.* An antecedent phrase sets up the expectation of some sort of resolution. A consequent phrase delivers that resolution.

Ex. 3.1.

Beethoven's "Ode to Joy"
Theme from the fourth movement of the ninth symphony

Composers such as Cole Porter, George Gershwin, Duke Ellington, Thomas "Fats" Waller, and Harold Arlen wrote songs that define the genre of the classic American song. That's why we use their songs as models. They wrote most of their songs in symmetric sections of equal-bar length—usually, four eight-bar sections. For example, the main part or *chorus* of George Gershwin's "I've Got Rhythm" has the form *AABA*. Look at the first eight bars of "I've Got Rhythm" and pay particular attention to the harmonic progression.

 "I've Got Rhythm" Harmonic Changes

Ex. 3.2.

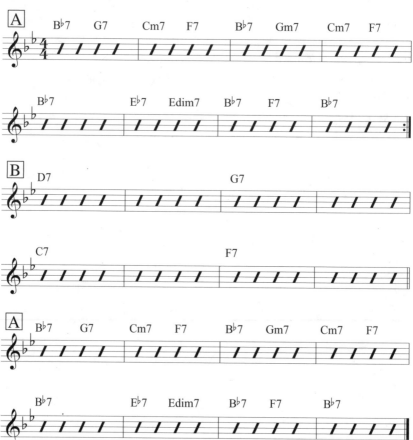

We'll call the first eight bars the *A* section and the second eight bars another *A* section because the harmonic progression and number of bars are exactly the same as the first section. In the third eight-bar section, there is new harmonic material we've not heard before, so we'll label that the *B* section. The last eight-bar section is an exact repetition of the first *A* section, so we'll again label it *A*. So, "I've Got Rhythm" is a 32-bar song and has a form of *AABA*.

Sometimes composers preface the main part or chorus of their songs with a *verse*. The purpose of a verse in a song is to lyrically set up the story, which will then be fully developed in the chorus. (In formal terms, think of the verse as an antecedent and the chorus as the consequent.) A verse is usually shorter than a chorus and is commonly omitted in performance.

Let's say we want to arrange the chorus of Gershwin's "I've Got Rhythm" and we want to write an original introduction and an ending. Does that change the form of Gershwin's song? No. The song still has an *AABA* form. We just added an introduction and an ending, changing the arrangement rather than the form.

It is your prerogative as an arranger to add any formal, harmonic, or melodic material to a song. Let's say we want to add a four-bar introduction and a four-bar ending to the song. The form of the arrangement now looks like this:

Introduction	A	A	B	A	Ending
Four bars	Eight bars	Eight bars	Eight bars	Eight bars	Four bars

Table 3.1. Form

The form of Gershwin's song is still *AABA*. Now, let's say we've arranged the song so that the melody and harmonies are presented in their original condition without any alteration. But the second time through the song, we'll want a different instrument to play the melody. Now the form of the arrangement looks like this:

Introduction, *AABA, AABA,* Ending

The form of the song is still AABA; we've just repeated it. What if we repeat it a third time? It might get a little tedious unless we do something different with the material. What can we do to the form that will add some interest to our arrangement? Let's add an *interlude.*

An interlude is a section placed in the middle of an arrangement designed to provide a dramatic diversion or a sense of transition. An interlude is usually composed of original musical material based on some part of the song's melody, harmony, or rhythmic motif. An interlude can be of any length but is usually around eight bars long. Sometimes it is used to facilitate a key change known as a *modulation.* Now the form of our arrangement looks like this:

Introduction, *AABA, AABA,* Interlude, *AABA,* Ending

HINT: If interludes are too long, they can confuse listeners—making them think that you've left the form of the song and gone off in some other direction. On the other hand, if they're too short, they sound like an unwelcome intrusion into an otherwise well-formed arrangement.

Form in Practice: Sequencing Your Arrangement

The starting point in sequencing an arrangement is deciding on the right tempo. Let's make sure we have a clear understanding of what tempo means. Tempo refers to the speed of the song and is expressed with metronome markings in terms of beats per minute, i.e., mm = 120 means 120 beats per minute.

Meter refers to the regularity of pulse within a given bar of music and is expressed in terms of a fraction—the numerator representing the number of beats or pulses in a single bar of music and the denominator indicating which metric unit will represent one beat. For example, a 6/8 time signature means there are six beats in every bar and the eighth note will represent a single beat.

A song can be in any meter regardless of its tempo. As a matter of practice, you should decide on your tempo before you start sequencing your song. I usually play the song a few times to get an idea of what tempo feels right, and then I begin to build my sequence.

Exactly how to sequence an arrangement depends a lot on the tempo and *feel* of the song. We'll examine the two most common tempo types:

Tempo Type 1

Songs with strict tempos, e.g. marches, most hymns, most jazz and pop music, dances, and so on.

Tempo Type 2

Songs that are *rhapsodic;* i.e., songs with no fixed meter whose time seems to vary from bar to bar.

Tempo-types will effect the way you sequence.

Tempo Type 1 Exercise

For this exercise, we'll sequence the song "O Tannenbaum," and we'll stay in tempo from the beginning to the end.

Choose Instrumentation

It's time to choose the instruments in our digital ensemble. Let's arrange our song for drums, bass, piano, and flute. Next, let's assign the instruments (programs) to their individual tracks.

IMPORTANT: The technical specifications for General MIDI dedicate MIDI Channel 10 to drum sounds. You must use MIDI Channel 10 for drums in the GM mode. On your sequencer, you can record GM drum parts on any track or tracks you like; you must first make sure those tracks are set to MIDI Channel 10. Consult your owner's manual to learn how channel assignment is done on your digital instrument.

Let's assume we have an 8-track sequencer. Record the piano accompaniment on Track 1, the acoustic bass on Track 2, the flute melody on Track 3, and the drums on Tracks 4 through 8.

HINT: Before you start sequencing your arrangement, I suggest you make a formal outline like the one below. That way, you'll be very clear on the form of your arrangement. You'll know exactly how many bars long your sequence will be, and it will be easier for you to keep track of which instruments you have playing in each section and any alterations you make as the arrangement progresses.

"O Tannenbaum" – for Flute, Piano, Acoustic Bass, Drums

Tempo: mm = 104

Intro	A	A	B	A	Interlude	B	A	Ending
4 bars	4 bars	4 bars	4 bars	4 bars	4 bars	4 bars	4 bars	4 bars
Rhythm Section & Flute	Flute, Piano Melody	Flute, Piano Melody	Flute, Melody	Flute, Piano Melody	Rhythm Section & Flute	Bass Plays Melody	Flute, Piano Melody	Rhythm Section & Flute

Table 3.2. Form and Instrumentation

Okay! You've chosen the instrumentation and tempo, and you've mapped out the form of your arrangement. You're ready to start sequencing. Here is how I arranged "O Tannenbaum."

NOTE: Music organized this way is called a *score*. A score makes it easy to see what all the instruments are doing at the same time. Some sequencing software is set up to look like a score. Although you don't have to write a real score when arranging in the digital domain, it does help to think this way.

44 *"O Tannenbaum" Arrangement*

Ex. 3.3.

"O Tannenbaum"–Score

Sequencing Procedure

"O Tannenbaum"

It may seem a little odd, but I started by sequencing the closed hi-hat part first without any melody or harmony. The closed hi-hat cymbal is the only part that plays all through the arrangement. Its function is to keep steady time on beats 2 and 4 from the beginning to the end of the arrangement. It acts like a very cool metronome. Since I mapped out the arrangement ahead of time, I knew how long each section was going to be.

Here's how I did it—step by step:

1. I turned on the built-in metronome on the digital keyboard set to a tempo of 104.

2. In the General MIDI mode, there is only one drum set available. I chose the closed hi-hat from that sound set to record first.

3. I pushed the record button and played the hi-hat on beats 2 and 4 on Track 5. To keep playing in time, I played the entire part with the built-in metronome running. Since you're going to rely on the hi-hat

to be your metronome, this is the only track you will need to *quantize*. So, even though you think you played the part flawlessly in tempo, take my advice—quantize it.

4. I turned off the internal metronome.

5. Then I recorded the piano accompaniment on Track 1, using the hi-hat on Track 5 as my metronome.

6. Next, I recorded the bass part on Track 2.

7. Then, I recorded the flute melody on Track 3. At this point, the foundation of the arrangement has been laid. The next step is to dress it up.

8. I recorded a ride cymbal part on Track 4.

9. I then erased and re-recorded the piano accompaniment part on Track 1. If possible, I always re-record an accompaniment part. It adds a live feel that you can't capture with the first recording because the other parts have not yet been recorded.

10. Finally, I backed up my work on a disk to protect it from damage or accidental erasure.

We ended up with a rather jazzy version of "O Tannenbaum." Why, do you suppose? Do you think it had something to do with the instrumentation?

Tempo Type 2 Exercise

For a rhapsodic sequence, it is often better to create an accompaniment using instruments that don't imply any kind of rhythm or fixed meter. For example, you could use cymbal roles, string or electronic pads, or other instrumental effects that act as a bed on which the melody can lie and don't restrict or confine the free flow of its expression.

Listen to this example.

 Rhapsodic Sequence

Notice how the percussion instruments I used do not imply any tempo or meter, but they dynamically support the contours of the melody.

CHAPTER IV
Sequencing Tips

To create successful, authentic-sounding sequences, you need to know a little bit about how the instrument you're trying to represent is actually played in its acoustic form. Piano players new to sequencing make a common mistake of playing every part as if they're playing a piano. The resulting sequence usually sounds too busy and cluttered. Using the *controllers* on your digital keyboard, such as *pitch bend* and *modulation,* helps lend authenticity to the parts. Several models of digital keyboards have velocity maps built into the programs that give the same note a different sound depending on how hard or at what *velocity* you strike the key. The most common example of this feature on digital keyboards is the electric bass sound. On many keyboards, if you choose an electric bass program and strike a key with a normal *velocity,* it will simply sound like an electric bass played normally. However, if you strike the key with a *forte* attack, you'll hear a slap bass percussive snap.

HINT: The ability to change tone color by velocity requires that you practice your keyboard technique. I suggest you play through all of your patches to find which sounds are altered by changes in velocity and get used to employing all the color possibilities your keyboard has to offer.

Wind Instruments

 Wind Instruments

If you're playing a flute, oboe, clarinet, bassoon, trumpet, trombone, or horn part, you must remember that these instruments can play only one note at a time. So, be careful not to suddenly play a chord in the middle of a long stretch of single notes. And speaking of long stretches of notes: Players of wind instruments have to breathe. I suggest that as you play a passage, exhale! When you need to take a breath, stop playing. You'll be surprised how much more effective your horn lines will be. Bending the pitch of a trombone with either a pitch-bend wheel, joystick, or ribbon can be a very satisfying effect. Warning: This can be overdone.

Guitar

I can't count the number of times I've seen someone choose a perfectly good guitar program on a digital keyboard, play Joplin's "Maple Leaf Rag," look me straight in the eye, and say, "This doesn't sound like a guitar!" The standard guitar has only six strings; on its best day, it can play only six notes simultaneously. Because of the way the six strings are tuned, *open voicings* are better than very *close voicings.* Generally speaking, a given guitar chord will contain only four or five notes. As a rule, to get a more authentic guitar sound, roll your chords. This will give you a strumming effect. Don't play all the notes of a guitar chord at once (as with a piano).

 Fret Noise & Pitch Bend

Here again, pitch bend can be a very handy effect, especially in rock and blues styles. If your digital keyboard is General MIDI compatible, within the GM sound set is a program called "fret noise." When a guitarist moves his left hand, there is a noise caused by the friction of the hand going over the strings. As you're sequencing an acoustic guitar part, simply add the fret noise sound on a separate track of your sequencer. You'll be amazed by how real it can sound.

Brass Sections

Because brass sections naturally sound dense, make sure your *voicings* aren't too thick. A standard brass section voicing has an interval of a tenth between the bottom two voices and either a *6/4 triad* in the top three voices or a chord voiced so that the interval of a sixth occurs in the top voices.

Brass Section Voicings

Ex. 4.1.

Brass stabs, which punctuate a phrase, are best when voiced higher (without the root in the bottom) and are best played with a very short *articulation*.

 Brass "Stabs"

Ex. 4.2.

Strings

Arranging for a real string section is an art with 400 years of tradition. No group of instruments I can think of possesses such a wide range of tone color and nuance as a string section. We are still many years away from truly emulating with a digital keyboard, all the tonal diversity a real string section has to offer. But, within a very narrow scope, we can satisfactorily replicate some string section clichés.

In general, when arranging for strings, less is more. I once wrote an article for *Keyboard* magazine in which I stated that in a pop music setting, it is very difficult to write bad music for strings. Nearly everything sounds good. Unfortunately, this is not true for the digital arranger. An overreliance on string pads will make an arrangement sound too thick and weigh it down. Single string lines that enter and exit throughout the course of an arrangement are more effective than ubiquitous string pads. A note of caution: When you introduce a single-line string part, be careful not to confuse the listener into thinking that the string line is the melody. A *counterline* should be played at a lower dynamic level than the melody, and it should be less rhythmically active. Avoid using low strings in a pad because this will always make your production sound muddy. In general, stick to violin parts.

If strings are used to articulate a chord progression, think of each note as part of an individual line. Keep in mind how each note leads to the next note and how it forms a line. Make sure the lines you create with this process don't leap around. Otherwise, the parts will sound disjunct. There is really no such thing as a typical string voicing because, as previously stated, string chords are usually the result of individual lines. However, when voicing strings, chords constructed in intervals of sixths are a good place to start. For example:

String Lines and Intervals

Ex 4.3.

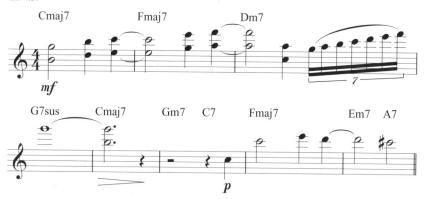

 Pizzicato Strings

Sometimes a *pizzicato,* or a plucked string, sound is used to add emphasis to melodic phrases. Usually pizzicato strings are unison, although not always.

Drums and Percussion

Finish tom-tom fills with a cymbal on beat 1.

 Tom-Tom Fills with Cymbal

Ex. 4.4.

Don't overplay percussion instruments. Once again, less is more. Develop specific patterns in each section and return to these patterns. This process gives continuity to the arrangement.

Quantizing Drums and Percussion

In swing music, I recommend quantizing only the hi-hat part and playing the other drum parts freely in time as best you can. Doing so has the effect of letting the other parts feel more natural and live.

With Latin or Brazilian music, I suggest that you quantize the hi-hat, bass drum, and the electric bass parts. This type of music requires a higher degree of accuracy in the underlying parts in order for the more surface-level parts, such as the conga and the cowbell, to sound flowing.

CHAPTER V
Production & MIDI

PRODUCTION

O nce the musical part of your arrangement is done, you'll want to add finishing touches to your sequence. The production values of a sequence are as important a factor in making your arrangement sound authentic as are your skills as a digital arranger. One of the more common tools you have at your disposal is reverb.

Reverb gives the listener a perception of depth by tricking the listener's ear into thinking that the music is being heard in an acoustic space other than the one it's actually in. Reverbs digitally recreate the acoustical properties of different types of rooms, right down to the materials from which these rooms are made. That's why reverb descriptions are typically Hall, Small Room, Cathedral, and so on.

Think of it: If you're in a gymnasium and you clap your hands, you'll hear the sound of that clap almost as you would an echo. Acousticians measure the time it takes from the moment you clap your hands for the sound to travel from your hands to the wall at the far end of the gym and back again in units called milliseconds. On your digital keyboard, you can recreate various environments and thereby give your music a sense of depth.

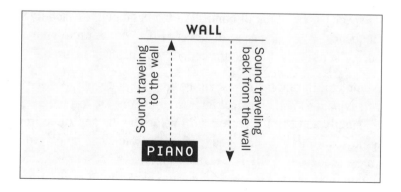

Fig. 5.1. Reverb

Most digital keyboards give you the ability to add and control the type and amount of reverb and effects you want. Some digital keyboards let you use only one type of reverb on the entire sequence; this is called a global reverb. Some allow you to use different reverbs on each individual track. Consult your owner's manual to learn how to assign reverb.

Panning gives the perception of placement within the stereo spectrum. Imagine your music being played by an ensemble on a stage. Not every musician plays in the center of the stage; some are in the middle, some are on the left, and some are on the right. Panning allows you to digitally recreate the physical placement of each instrument in your virtual ensemble, thereby giving your sequence the sense of width.

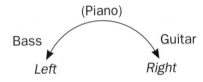

Fig. 5.2. Panning

MIDI CONTROLLERS

MIDI controllers are like virtual conductors who have the responsibility of controlling the expression of your music. By inserting MIDI controller numbers (which identify the type of controller) and values (which specify the amount of control) at the beginning of each track of your sequence, you will ensure that every time you return to your sequence, the proper sounds at the proper volumes will be used.

For example, if during the course of a sequence you want to make dynamic changes to add musical interest or expression to your performance, simply add MIDI Controller 7 (Volume) with any value from 0 (being no sound) to 127 (being as loud as the sound can be played.) With most sequencers, MIDI controller numbers with their values can be inserted on a given track the same way you record note information. A chart of MIDI controller numbers and their functions follows.

Common MIDI controllers and their functions:

MIDI Controller 7:	Volume	values range from 0 to 127
MIDI Controller 10:	Pan	values range from 0, hard right, to 127, hard left
MIDI Controller 32:	Bank select	(see page 2)
MIDI Controller 64:	Sustain pedal	values are either ON or OFF
MIDI Controller 66	Sostenuto pedal	values are either ON or OFF
MIDI Controller 67:	Soft pedal	values are either ON or OFF
MIDI Controller 1:	Modulation wheel	values range from 0 to 127
MIDI Controller 11:	Expression	values range from 0 to 127

Table 5.1. Common MIDI Controllers

You should also get in the habit of inserting patch-change numbers with volume (Controller 7) information at the beginning of every track of every sequence you do. Most sequencers in digital keyboards do this work for you. If you're using a software-based or stand-alone sequencer, here's a tip:

> Place patch-change numbers, volume commands (Controller 7 with some value), *sysex* information, and any other MIDI information in a set-up measure (one that contains no notes) before the sequence begins. Doing so allows the digital instrument(s) you're working with to be set up before the actual note information is played. Failing to put this information in a count-off measure can cause an audible glitch in the music, because the sequencer tries to play the note information while calling up the proper patches and volumes. Controller information in the count-off measure sets everything up before the sequence plays the notes.

You can record the controller information one increment at a time or you can use a *continuous controller* device such as a pedal, a wheel, a slider, a joystick, or a strip to enter the information. Generally speaking, recording information that creates subtle changes over time—as do *crescendos, diminuendos, accelerandos,* and *ritardandos*—is best recorded with continuous controller devices.

You can record continuous controller information one of two ways:

1. *Overdub* the information directly onto the track you want to be affected.

2. Create a new track and assign it to the same MIDI channel as the track containing the notes you want to be affected. This method is marginally safer because you don't run any risk of erasing the note information you've already recorded.

CHAPTER VI
Conclusion and Assignments

As with any skill, sequencing requires practice in order to improve. The hints I gave you, such as cataloging your patches and relating your bass and drum parts, will save you production time and make your sequences sound more authentic. But you'll still have to spend a lot of time at the controls in order to really understand what you're asking your sequencer and digital instrument to do. To that end, let me revert back to my teaching days and give you a couple of assignments.

Assignment 1

Listen to a variety of musical styles. If you normally listen to country music, listen to jazz for one week, the next week listen to rock. While you're listening, don't think about why you don't like this or that style; be analytical. Think about how the music works. "What instruments are used? How are they being used? In what ranges are they played?" Identify the common accompaniment patterns and licks they play. Find the patches on your digital keyboard that sound the closest to the instruments you heard and try to reproduce their parts exactly. This will help you to develop new performance techniques and accurately replicate instruments.

Assignment 2

Choose a song you know and arrange it in a style in which you've NOT heard that song played before. Remember the order of good sequencing:

1. Choose the song.

2. Decide on the tempo.

3. Determine the orchestration.

4. Map out your arrangement.

5. Lay out your tracks.

6. Begin recording.

7. Back up your work.

PRACTICAL APPLICATIONS

I n the Introduction, I mentioned that teachers, church musicians, and gigging musicians could all benefit from this book. Here are some other practical applications. The possibilities seem endless.

Ideas for music teachers

1. Composition teachers can use a sequencer as a digital scratch pad to help their students learn voice-leading principles, counterpoint, form, and orchestration. Digitally orchestrate a passage from a well-known score, and then re-orchestrate it. Help your students discover why certain choices were made.

2. Record a sequence of a contrapuntal passage by Bach, Mozart, or Beethoven where each line is played by a patch of contrasting instrumental color. The mysteries of counterpoint become more quickly understandable this way.

3. For music appreciation, history, or style analysis classes, sequence the first few bars of your favorite works and examine their construction, orchestration, and harmony.

4. Create games that are really rhythmic drills. Use the variety of sounds on your digital keyboard to bring new life to potentially boring exercises. Use the quantize feature as an auditory development tool to help your students identify and correct inaccuracies in their performance.

Ideas for church musicians

1. You can shorten the time it takes your choir members to learn their parts by sequencing their vocal parts. Sequence the soprano part on Track 1 using a flute patch, the alto part on Track 2 using a clarinet patch, the tenor part on Track 3 using a cello patch, and the bass part on Track 4 using a tuba patch. Recording individual parts this way makes it easier for singers to hear and learn their parts because each part sounds distinct.

2. If you direct a small choir, sequencing the hymn using a big voice patch mixed in with another instrument patch, such as organ or piano, will make your choir sound huge.

3. If you are the church musician and you have to be away some particular Sunday, you can sequence and store your service ahead of time.

4. If you have a traveling ministry and sing at many different locations, you know you can't count on consistent quality from various accompanists. By having your accompaniments sequenced, you can have dependable accuracy.

5. There are thousands of titles—both traditional and contemporary—for every denomination available commercially on disk in the General MIDI format. Having access to such a huge amount of repertoire can make your sequencing life a lot easier and your performances very diverse and exciting.

Ideas for gigging musicians

Think of your digital keyboard and sequencer as the tools that make the first step of producing your own CD possible. Recently, the sound quality and production values available to the amateur musician have risen to the professional standard. There is essentially no difference between what you can do at home and what is done at a professional recording studio. If you want to add acoustic instruments or voices to the virtual tracks you've already sequenced, you can transfer your sequenced tracks to a multitrack digital tape recorder such as the Alesis ADAT or a Tascam DA-88 and gain that flexibility. These 8-track digital recording devices enable you to record a stereo version of your sequence on two tracks and record acoustic instruments, vocals, or other sounds not available on your keyboard or digital sound source on the remaining tracks. This route is more expensive because it requires using more equipment that you would have to buy or rent, and it presupposes the eventual involvement of a recording studio.

There are many demo projects and, indeed, finished CDs currently for sale that have been produced with nothing more than a single digital keyboard and a sequencer. Music technology advances with blinding speed and unfailing regularity. Waiting for the next generation of device or gadget to arrive is almost never a good idea. Don't get bogged down in the technology; it's only there to help you.

The last group I mentioned in my introduction is made up of those people for whom music is a passion. This group, in which I include myself, is the reason I wrote this book. And so, fellow passionate musicians, I conclude with this wish: that this book will help bring a new depth to your arranging and thereby foster a greater appreciation of your music.

Happy sequencing!

LISTENING LIST

This list is designed to help you broaden your listening habits and make you more aware of styles you might otherwise not be inclined to seek out. It comes from my own library of records and CDs and is only a reflection of what I like and feel comfortable recommending to you.

Artist	Album/CD Title
Eddie Palmieri	*El Rumbero del Piano*
Tony Bennet and Bill Evans	*Again*
Shania Twain	*Come On Over*
The Manhattan Transfer	*The Christmas Album*
Shirley Horn	*Here's to Life*
Dianne Reeves	*Quiet After the Storm*
Miles Davis	*My Funny Valentine* *Porgy and Bess* *Sketches of Spain*
Pat Metheny	*Letter from Home*
Lyle Lovett	*His Large Band*
Gal Costa	*Personalidade*
Buckwheat Zydeco	*Taking It Home*
James Taylor	*Mudslide Slim and the Blue Horizon*
Frank Sinatra	anything arranged by Nelson Riddle
Count Basie	*April in Paris*
Enio Morricone	*Cinema Paradiso* (soundtrack) *Bugsy* (soundtrack)

Artist	Album/CD Title
Asleep At The Wheel	*Western Standard Time*
Luther Vandross	*Power of Love*
Louis Jordan	*Rock and Roll*
Nat Cole	*Lush Life*
Clifton Chenier	*Frenchin' the Boogie*
Garth Brooks	*Sevens*
Faith Hill	*Faith*
João Gilberto	*The Legendary João Gilberto*
Billie Holiday	*The Quintessential Billie Holiday*
Django Reinhardt and Stephan Grapelli	anything from *The Hot Club of Paris*
Annie Ross	*A.R. Sings a Song with Mulligan*
Lambert, Hendricks and Ross	*Twisted: The Best of L. H. and R.*
BeBe and CeCe Winans	*Heaven*
Astor Piazzolla	*The Central Park Concert*
Patsy Cline	*Patsy Cline*
Donald Fagen	*The Nightfly*
Jean-Luc Ponty	*Tchokola*
Dori Caymmi	*Apassionata*
Art Tatum	any solo piano recording
Fletcher Henderson	*Developing an American Orchestra*
Coleman Hawkins	*Body and Soul*
Igor Stravinsky	*Petroushka* *The Firebird*

Artist	Album/CD Title
Bela Bartók	*Music for Strings, Percussion and Celesta* *String Quartet Nos. 4 and 5*
Maurice Ravel	*String Quartet in F* *Trio for Piano, Violin, and Cello*
Modeste Mussorgsky	*Pictures at an Exhibition* (orchestration by Ravel)
Dmitri Shostakovich	*Piano Concerto No. 2 in F*
Wolfgang Amadeus Mozart	*Symphony Nos. 40 and 41*
Fats Waller	Piano Solos
Dave Grusin	*The Milagro Beanfield Wars* (soundtrack) *The Gershwin CD*
Richard Wagner	*Siegfried Idyll* *Overture to Tristan and Isolde*
Ravi Shankar	*The Sounds of India*
Peter I. Tchaikovsky	*Symphony No. 5*
Robert Schumann	*Symphony No. 3*
Felix Mendelssohn	*Symphony No. 3* *Violin Concerto in E Minor*
Gustav Mahler	*Das Lied Von Der Erde*
Charles Ives	*George Washington's Birthday*
Thad Jones/Mel Lewis	any recording featuring their big band

GLOSSARY

6/4 triad: The 6/4 inversion of a chord occurs when the 5th of the chord is in the bass and the remaining notes of the chord (the root and 3rd) form the intervals of a fourth and a sixth above.

accelerando: A gradual increase in tempo over time.

articulation: The way a note is played, e.g. short, long, or detached from or slurred into surrounding notes.

antecedent/consequent phrase: Customarily, an antecedent phrase creates an expectation of resolution because its cadence sounds incomplete. A consequent phrase completes the musical sentence by declaring a clear, definitive cadence.

arco: Played with a bow.

changes: Jazz musicians' jargon referring to the harmonic progression of a piece of music.

chorus: The main and often most familiar part of a song.

closed: Most often, the sound of a hi-hat cymbal when the foot pedal is held down. It produces a dry, somewhat stopped sound. It is notated with a plus sign (+) over the note. It can also refer to other cymbals and triangle parts.

continuous controller: A device such as a pedal, ribbon, or slider that sends a steady stream of controller information rather than a single command.

controller: Digital command that affects the note information in a sequence.

counterline: A secondary melody employed to act as a counterpoint to the primary melody, thereby adding drama and interest to the arrangement. It is often scored in a different register and played at a lower dynamic level than the primary melody.

crescendo: A gradual increase in volume.

diminuendo: A gradual decrease in volume.

feel: A general term commonly used to describe the rhythmic subtlety desired in a performance, e.g., a bossa-nova feel or a country feel.

forte: Loud.

groove: A slightly more specific term used to instruct a rhythm section how to play, e.g., a swing groove or a '50s rock-and-roll groove.

hardware: The physical devices necessary to implement musical applications of the software, e.g., keyboards and MIDI interfaces.

interlude: A short to medium-length insertion of musical material placed between sections of a longer musical work or between repetitions of standard song forms. Interludes are usually employed to add drama or to facilitate more structural events such as modulations or vastly different treatments of adjoining sections.

ledger lines: The lines drawn above or below a staff to accommodate notes that are either too high or too low to fit on the staff.

lick: Jazz jargon for a short melodic, harmonic, rhythmic, or even orchestrative phrase. A lick often begins as a musical signature of its author, e.g., Count Basie's ending lick. If a lick is accepted and imitated often enough, it can become a building block of a style.

modulation (controller): One wave form that controls some aspect (volume, pitch, panning) of a second waveform. With keyboards, the most common use is to control the volume or pitch resulting in a vibrato-like effect.

modulation (harmonic): The changing of tonal center (key) within a piece of music.

multi-timbral: Usually, the ability of a keyboard to play more than one sound at a time.

open: Usually, the sound of a hi-hat cymbal played without the foot pedal depressed. The cymbals are allowed to vibrate freely. It is notated with a small "○" over the note. It can also refer to other cymbals and triangle parts.

open/close voicings: A close voicing means that as many of the notes of the chord as possible are assembled within one octave. Conversely, an open voicing means that the notes of a chord are spread out. The degree to which they're spread out is determined by instrumentation, musical context, and taste.

ostinato: A clearly defined melodic or rhythmic phrase that is persistently repeated.

overdub: The act of recording over pre-recorded material.

pad: An accompaniment, usually strings, voices, or some thick-sounding synthesizer patch that is rhythmically static—it generally moves only to define the harmony and is harmonically very clearly defined.

panning: In recorded music, the virtual placement from left to right of instruments and voices in the stereo spectrum.

patch number: A number to which a synthesizer sound is assigned.

pitch bend: A digital effect triggered by some continuous controller device that either raises or lowers the pitch of a note.

pizzicato: Plucked, as in a string instrument.

program/patch: Synthesizer sounds.

quantize: An electronic process that realigns the attacks of notes so that they conform to an exact rhythmic grid. One can usually choose to quantize to the nearest sixteenth, eighth, eighth-note triplet, quarter, quarter-note triplet, half, or whole note.

reverb: Short for "reverberation," it is a sonic effect meant to recreate the properties of diverse acoustic settings.

rhapsodic: Somewhat free, out of time, not played in a rigid tempo.

ritardando: A gradual decrease in tempo.

score: The notation showing all the parts of an ensemble.

software: The commands written in some computer language that tell a computer what functions to perform.

sysex: Any feature exclusive to your model of digital instrument is called a "system exclusive" feature: "sysex" is an abbreviation. As with anything MIDI, there is a controller number and a value associated with each sysex feature. However, these controller numbers are by definition not standardized because they're only relevant to a specific instrument.

tone generator: A device that produces wave-forms, such as a synthesizer, or reproduces samples, such as sample playback.

velocity: A measure—in MIDI terms, 0 to127—of how hard a key on a keyboard is struck.

velocity maps: Some synthesizer programs are designed to play different sounds depending on the velocity with which the key is pressed. For example, a trumpet section program might play normally when it receives a velocity reading from 1 to 85. If it reads a velocity reading from 86 to 127, it might play a fall-off. Each program is designed with a velocity map.

verse: Lyrically establishes a story, which is then developed in the main part or chorus of the song. A verse is usually shorter than a chorus and, unless the arrangement calls for it, it is commonly omitted in performance.

voicing: The vertical ordering of the notes in a chord.

RANGE CHARTS

K now the actual range of the instrument you're trying to represent and make sure the parts you play don't exceed those limits. This range chart shows the actual range of the instruments related to your keyboard. Because you'll be playing them on a digital keyboard, don't take transpositions into account. In the case of strings, I am only concerned with the string section and not each individual instrument. Therefore, I give the range of the entire section.

Note: These ranges are a little narrower than the actual instrument's range. Keeping within these boundaries will make sure the parts sound authentic.

PICCOLO

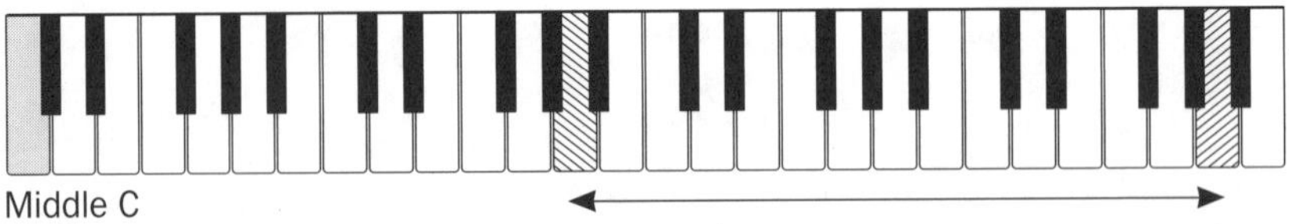

Middle C

FLUTE

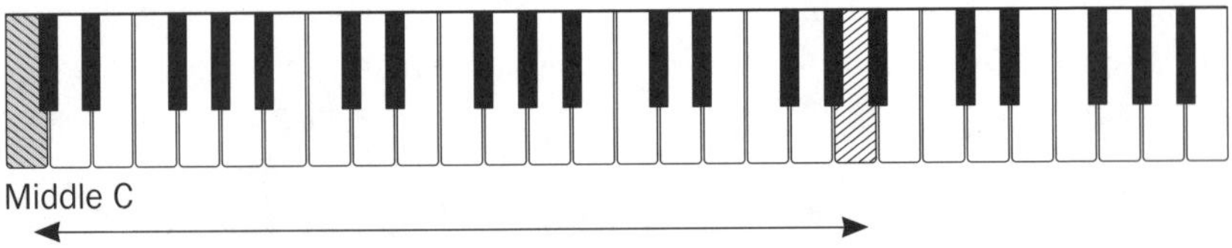

Middle C

OBOE

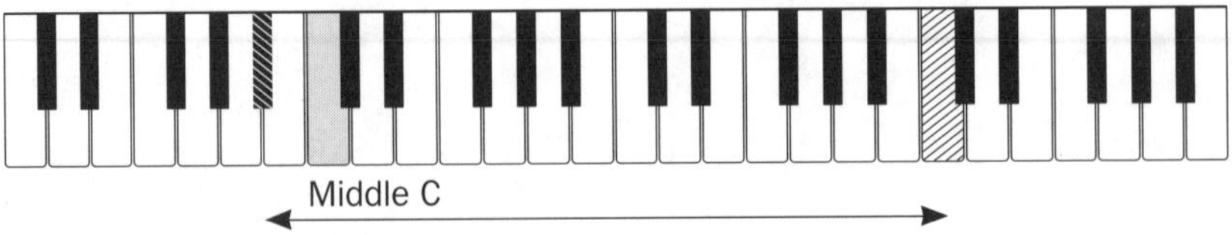

Middle C

BASSOON

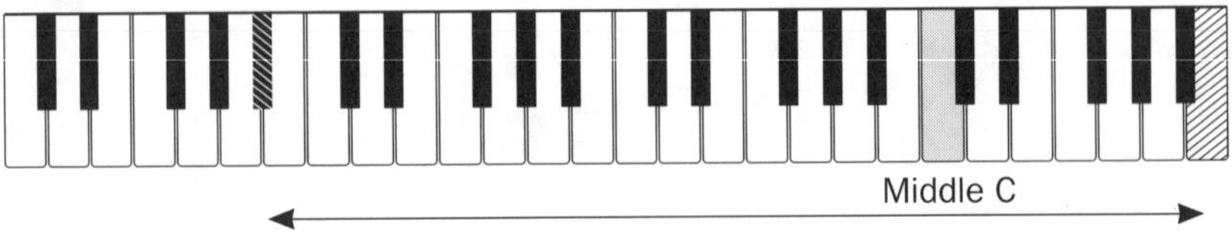

Middle C

CLARINET

Middle C

BASS CLARINET

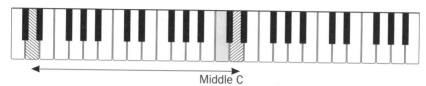

Middle C

SOPRANO SAX

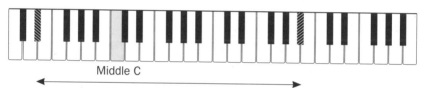

Middle C

ALTO SAX

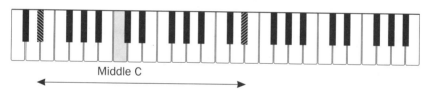

Middle C

TENOR SAX

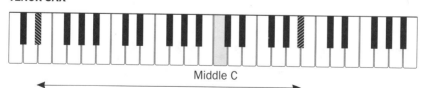

Middle C

BARITONE SAX

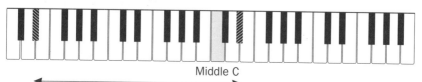

Middle C

TRUMPET

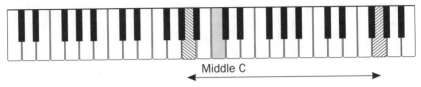

Middle C

FRENCH HORN

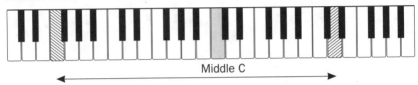

Middle C

TROMBONE

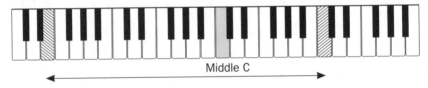

Middle C

STRINGS

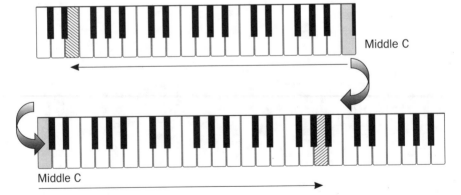

Middle C

Middle C

HARP

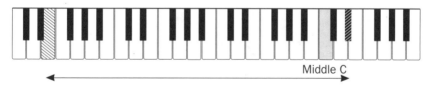

Middle C

Middle C

GUITAR

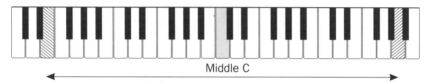

Middle C

ACOUSTIC AND ELECTRIC BASS

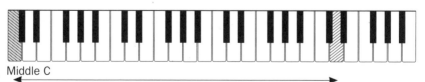

Middle C

HARMONICA

Middle C

ABOUT THE AUTHOR

Corey Allen's professional background covers the entire spectrum of the music business. As a record producer/arranger/keyboardist, Corey works with some of the biggest names in the music business: The Manhattan Transfer, Chuck Mangione, Dianne Reeves, Kim Basinger, Doc Severinson, Indeya, Suzanne Ciani, Peter Gordon, David Hasselhoff, and many others. Corey taught at the Berklee College of Music and continues to produce, arrange, and perform concerts internationally for Kurzweil Music Systems.

These books feature
material developed at the
Berklee College of Music

Visit www.berkleepress.com

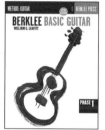

JIM KELLY'S GUITAR WORKSHOP SERIES

Jim Kelly's Guitar Workshop products are an integrated, interactive, instructional approach to helping guitarists improve their playing through songs and studies in jazz, blues, Latin, R&B, and more. The songs that Jim Kelly has written for this series are designed to help you learn how to play in the style of guitar greats like Jeff Beck, Kenny Burrell, Mike Stern, Pat Metheny, Wes Montgomery, Joe Pass, Stevie Ray Vaughan, and others. Listen to Jim capture the sound of these players, and then use the play-along tracks to develop your own approaches.

With full-band and play-along tracks, learn how to phrase your own solos in new ways by using the techniques of master guitar players.

Valuable to players at all levels, the strong melodies and chord changes are fun to listen to and learn. Jim and his band knock-out each tune so you can hear how it sounds featuring quartet and trio tracks with alto sax, acoustic and electric guitars, bass, and drums. The books provide you with traditional lead sheet music notation and guitar tablature, including style, tempo, form, fingerings, song description, as well as commentary, hints, tips, approach, and practice ideas.

Jim Kelly's Guitar Workshop DVD
63003162 DVD/Booklet.......................................$29.95

Jim Kelly's Guitar Workshop
00695230 Book/CD..$14.95

More Guitar Workshop by Jim Kelly
00695306 Book/CD..$14.95

Jim Kelly's Guitar Workshop Video
00320144 Video/Booklet.....................................$19.95

More Guitar Workshop Video, by Jim Kelly
00320158 Video/Booklet.....................................$19.95

BUSINESS GUIDES

The Self-Promoting Musician
by Peter Spellman
From the Director of Career Development at Berklee College of Music, learn how to become a success in the music business. Complete with tips for writing business plans and press kits; business know-how; using the Internet to promote music; customizing demos for maximum exposure; getting music played on college radio; and a comprehensive musician's resource list.
50449423 Book...$24.95

Prices and availability subject to change without notice.

Complete Guide to Film Scoring
by Richard Davis

Learn the art and business of film scoring, including: the film-making process; preparing and recording a score; contracts and fees; publishing, royalties, and copyrights. Features interviews with 19 film-scoring professionals.

50449417 Book...$24.95

Melody in Songwriting
by Jack Perricone

Learn the secrets to writing truly great songs. Unlike most songwriting books, this guide uses examples of HIT SONGS in addition to proven tools and techniques for writing memorable, chart-topping songs. Explore popular songs and learn what makes them work.

50449419 Book...$19.95

The New Music Therapist's Handbook – 2nd Edition
by Suzanne B. Hanser

Dr. Hanser's well respected *Music Therapist's Handbook* has been thoroughly updated and revised to reflect the latest developments in the field of music therapy. Includes: an introduction to music therapy; new clinical applications and techniques, case studies; designing, implementing, and evaluating individualized treatment programs, including guidelines for beginning music therapists.

50449424 Book...$29.95

Music Notation
by Mark McGrain

Learn the essentials of music notation, from pitch and rhythm placement to meter and voicing alignments. Excellent resource for both written and computer notation software.

50449399 Book...$19.95

Managing Lyric Structure
by Pat Pattison

This book will help songwriters handle lyric structures more effectively. Equally helpful to both beginning and experienced lyricists, this book features exercises that help you say things better and write better songs.

50481582 Book...$11.95

Masters of Music Conversations with Berklee Greats
by Mark Small and Andrew Taylor

An impressive collection of personal interviews with music industry superstars from *Berklee Today*, the alumni magazine of Berklee College of Music. Read about how these luminaries got their breaks, and valuable lessons learned along the way. Paula Cole talks about navigating through the recording industry, George Martin on technology's effect on artistic freedom, Patty Larkin considers the creative process, and Alf Clausen discusses scoring *The Simpsons*. Get the story from these stars and many others.

50449422 Book...$24.95

Rhyming Techniques and Strategies
by Pat Pattison

Find better rhymes and use them more effectively. If you have written lyrics before, even professionally, and you crave more insight and control over your craft, this book is for you. Beginners will learn good habits and techniques and how to avoid common mistakes.

50481583 Book...$10.95

Prices and availability subject to change without notice.

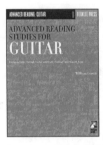